EMPOWERISM

A Guide to Lifestyle and Environmental Ethics

by
Christopher Mark D'Souza

MATRIX
PRODUCTIONS

First printing 2001

Printed on recycled paper

ISBN 0-9689247-0-0

Design and Book Production:
    Matrix Productions Limited
    www.selfpublishyourbook.com

This book has been self-published and self-financed. If you can offer any assistance with distribution and/or a publishing deal, please contact The Empowerists' Network by e-mail at chrismarkdsouza@hotmail.com.

The Empowerists' Network
6 Harridine Road
Brampton,
Ontario, Canada
L6X 3N8

Printed in Canada

PROLOGUE

In the summer of 1995, deep in the heart of the Sumatran rainforest, I held hands with a "wild" orangutan. He had been a prisoner of human captivity many years before, but was now living freely in the jungle, as God had originally intended for his species. His freedom was the result of an Indonesian initiative that was reintroducing these great apes into protected habitats, (after removing them by armed force from their incarceration). To say that this moment was an epiphany is an understatement. I realized that a group of individuals were successfully reversing the damage that humans had incurred on Mother Earth. And as that gentle, but powerful orange hand carefully grasped mine, I knew that I too had to strive to make a difference. The philosophy that unfolds in the following pages is a manifestation of that experience and many other natural encounters with the magnificent creatures with whom we share the earth. We must live every moment of our lives in harmony with the environment and challenge ourselves and others to minimize the impact we have on its delicate balance. In doing so, we will empower ourselves on a spiritual level and perpetuate a cycle of constant respect for ourselves and the earth.

CONTENTS

PART I

EMPOWERISM:
The Ideology

INTRODUCTION

*"Our greatest fear is not that we are inadequate;
Our greatest fear is that we are powerful beyond
measure ..."*

NELSON MANDELA

Empowerism is NOT a religion. It is a **Lifestyle Management Plan** that individuals can adopt to enhance their existence while striving to live in harmony with the environment and to foster an understanding that everything comes from Mother Earth and must be respected. The ultimate goal is to take charge of your life so that you can maintain optimal physical, emotional, mental and spiritual health and make a positive contribution to the environmental movement. (The philosophy itself has the potential to become a grass roots *tour de force.*)

None of the philosophy behind Empowerism is completely original. It is a simple compilation of many old ideas, recombined to aid us in our struggle with the complexities of the modern world. It is up to the proponent of Empowerism, called an Empowerist, to pick and choose the ideas that will best aid him/her to cope with daily life. There are no hard and fast doctrines, rules, or time consuming rituals. Incorporating Empowerism into your life will aid in your spiritual journey, emotional and physical health, relationships and daily routine. Empowerists strive to become "Empowered". The goal is to incorporate as many ideas as possible to heighten your level of empowerment and ultimately minimize your impact on the environment until that impact is negligible.

"Immorality, no less than morality, has at all times found support in religion."

SIGMUND FREUD

Old World religions are being ignored by modern humanity because humans have chosen to focus their attention on material distractions, rather than spiritual needs. The high speed of technological advancements, the global village, the destruction of Mother Earth and the seemingly limitless access to information did not exist when Christ preached, Buddha philosophized and Mohammed taught. Empowerism recognizes that what these three individuals espoused was indeed true and divine, but over the centuries humans have manipulated their ideals to meet their own needs and in essence, have diluted the original divinity of those teachings.

Empowerism will enable the modern individual to meet the demands of the Third Millenium while maintaining a strong devotion to the religion of their birth or conversion or an entirely new spirituality could be discovered within themselves that might never have existed before.

CHAPTER ONE

EMPOWERISM: Basic Concepts

"I believe in the intrinsic goodness of humanity
... but belief is not enough!"
CHRISTOPHER MARK D'SOUZA

1. Always think positively. This is the most difficult dogma of Empowerism, but as you embrace the lifestyle, it will get easier to believe in the beauty of life, the greatness of God and the magnificence of the natural world that has been given to us. If you have empowered yourself, every moment is indeed positive. A major goal of Empowerism is to eradicate negativity and to make the individual aware of how truly simple it is to become a force that can live harmoniously with the earth.

2. Recognize your humanness. Focus on your power to feel. Strive to be a role model to others every waking moment of your life.

3. Live in harmony with the natural world around you. Be sensitive to the environment and respect everything it provides for your daily existence.

4. Consume only what you need.

5. Believe in peace. Adhere to its promises. Fight for it.

The following chapters provide strategies that you can incorporate into your life to empower yourself, the people around you and the environment that is your life support system.

Spirituality

In most regions of the world, one's culture and/or race dictate one's religion. Unfortunately, many individuals become detached from their initial beliefs because of rigid rules and value systems that are imposed upon them, eventually causing them to become apathetic about their religion.

We cannot prove the existence of God, but proof is not important. Belief in a higher power is simply understood (because of the intrinsic beauty of the natural world around us) and it is therefore unnecessary to waste time trying to prove or disprove any potential theories. You must focus on what you can verify. YOU exist! Your family and friends exist as well as the environment around you. They must all be nurtured in order for you to be empowered. Buddhism, although a wonderful way of life, makes the claim that there is no true self or *atman*. Instead, it teaches that we are a part of one life force. (I personally believe that Siddartha Gautama, the Buddha, did truly reach enlightenment, but such a level of spirituality is almost impossible to attain in modern society. How many of us have time to meditate for hours a day? Much of the eight-fold path, the Buddhist doctrine that dictates life, is reflected in Empowerism but in a manner that is practical for day-to-day life in the third millenium.)

Empowerists need to shed the archaic belief that humans were given dominion over nature and that they are the dominant creatures, with liberty to use the earth's resources in excess of their needs. Our spirituality must be derived from the simple pleasures of life: friends, family, clean living, exhaltation in nature, planting a tree, attaining personal goals and basking in the beauty of the natural world that God has created. Individuals of any faith background can adopt the philosophy of Empowerism.

The Environment

Empowerists could care less about Apathy

"The global village", a catch phrase coined by media guru
Marshall McLuhan in the 1960's, suggests that the world is one
community. The cross-cultural transfer of ideas is not a new
concept. There is speculation that Christ encountered Buddhist
philosophy during the twenty or so odd years that the New
Testament does not chronicle, and then incorporated it into his
teachings. This exchange of knowledge is as old as language
itself. It is the speed and range of the exchange, however, (which
is increasing at exponential rates) that exemplifies the Third
Millenium. Communication happens instantly and in real time
worldwide. But with such progress comes a huge responsibility
because we now have irrefutable knowledge: MOTHER EARTH
IS DYING! And we are her Executioner.

Statistics on global pollution, global warming, destruction
of the ozone, damage to rain-forests, and the systematic extinction of animal species provide a terrifying record of
humankind's legacy. In 1992, ten Noble Peace Prize winners pre-
dicted that catastrophic environmental disasters were a mere
ten years away. They were correct in their results. In 1997, a 1%
increase in the earth's global temperature caused the bleaching
of over 70% of the coral reefs in our living seas. In this new millenium, only one-tenth of the forest covering the earth remains
and over half the species have become extinct.

There is no excuse for inaction. In the past we claimed
ignorance because of lack of substantial data. But we now have
irrefutable information, along with video and satellite pictorial
proof. For too long, nature and all of its resources have been
viewed as commodities to be consumed by humans. Living

species need to be respected for the simple reason that they are alive and not because they could potentially serve a purpose to humanity now or in the future.

All of our existence is intrinsically linked to the health of our environment; hence, we are empowered by it. In his book *Naked Ape to Super-species,* Canadian geneticist and world renowned environmentalist David Suzuki, explains that the problem with continuous growth is that, as the science of physics tells us, we live in a closed system with respect to matter (natural materials). For example, we cannot have a systematic deterioration of the productivity of nature, species diversity, and still maintain the ecosphere's abundance. In order to have a chance of acting sustainably, we need a society that is just, equitable and distributes resources fairly. Without such a society, some people will take far too much while others become so desperate that they will chop down the last trees or use up the last drops of water.

Nothing in nature grows forever except cancer cells, and they too will die when they have killed their host. Apathy is the global cancer spreading across its host, Mother Earth. Empowerists must make it their goal to revolt against this apathy. The problem is indeed enormous, but not unsolvable.

The Afterlife

*"To emphasize the afterlife is to deny life. To con-
centrate on heaven is to create hell."*
TOM ROBBINS, U.S. Writer

Modern technological advancements in medicine may one day
cure all forms of diseases that presently kill human beings.
Proper research on dietary habits and nutrition is resulting in
the eradication of free radicals, chemical agents that cause aging
in our bodies, and therefore, might extend our life-span to ages
never imagined. We might even travel to Mars and move at the
speed of light, but it is widely understood that we will never
solve the mystery of what happens to us after death. Theories
of reincarnation, heaven, nirvana and enlightenment are all
beautiful but they are the result of a human egocentrism that
refuses to believe that we might cease to exist after our bodies
stop functioning.

Empowerism offers up no new theory for this unsolvable
mystery. It does suggest though that Empowerists spend their
energies on what is real and in front of them. Too many people
spend so much of their time worrying about the afterlife that
they miss the beauty of the "now life". Enjoy today and remi-
nisce fondly about yesterday. Plan for tomorrow. Live in
harmony with the environment so that there will be a future for
your children and their great-grandchildren's children. **Leave
the afterlife to God!**

CHAPTER TWO

The Lifestyle

Three mind-sets are particularly important ...
First, the understanding that each of us is truly
part of an extended family that includes people
every place and also extends in time to include
all who will ever be born. We have a responsi-
bility to those family members separated from
us by centuries. Second, that equity is more than
just important ... it is indeed the basis for the
Golden Rule. We can't allow ourselves to enjoy
the benefits of the world with the poverty of the
poor actually subsidizing our enjoyment. Third,
it is important to understand that interdepen-
dence goes beyond the human race. Everything
affects everything, and just as hairspray used in
the Western Hemisphere has had effects on the
ozone layer and health throughout the world, so
does the health of the African continent have
direct impact on North America.

JIMMY CARTER

Empowerism demands that every individual exist in harmonious
conjunction with the environment. It does not dictate the abo-
lition of all material wealth or extreme vegetarianism (vegan-
ism), but a respect for nature, a reduction of consumption,
recycling whenever possible and the cessation of unnecessary
waste. Vicki Robin, author of *Your Money or Your Life*, says that
" ... Everything we interact with on a daily basis comes out of

the Earth and goes back to the Earth [usually in the form of a contaminant] and deserves to be treated with tremendous appreciation, gratitude and respect. This awareness, rather than create a sense of guilt, should incite gratitude." Think how lucky you are, how lucky we all are, to have these simple things to make our lives easier. The more gratitude you feel for things that you have, the less you're going to be inclined to over-consume. Once you have something you really like and enjoy, be sure to really like and enjoy it and do so for many years. And when you have to get rid of it, make sure you put it in a place where other people can like and enjoy it as well. Doing so is really an appreciation of the material world, and an honouring of the life energy that it took for you to purchase that thing, and also the life energy it took from the Earth to create it.

Before purchasing or consuming something, Empowerists must always ask themselves: **Do I really need this?** And if you really do, then take it and enjoy it. But if you can do without it, then that should be the option you exercise. For example, when you go to your local fast-food restaurant and purchase a drink, do you really need a straw? This optional item, even though it is free, is made of plastic, an extremely toxic material when it finally breaks down in landfills. It might make the consumption of your beverage a little easier for the 5-6 minutes you use it, but it will then lie in a landfill for centuries. Empowerists will endure the inconvenience of removing the plastic lid and sipping directly from the cup. For that matter, why not eliminate the lid too? It seems like a small (and simple thing to do) but imagine if everyone around you did the same thing, and then applied this thinking to their consumption of plastic utensils, napkins, condiment containers, etc.? Eventually, the restaurant could save money and potentially transfer these savings to the customer.

"Chicken Soul for the Soup?"

Dietary Habits

Empowerists should work toward a goal of at least three days of vegetarianism per week. Reducing meat from your diet is good for the individual and reduces the demand on the environment. Soy, for example, requires 70% less crop space to produce the same amount of protein as beef. Therefore, an acre of soy provides three and a half times more protein than an acre used for cattle grazing.

Start slowly. Incorporate one meal a day and then progress to three to four meals per week. The ultimate goal should be that you are practising vegetarianism three to four full days a week.

● Research how to minimize meat consumption by "volumizing" meals with tofu. For example, you can halve the amount of ground beef used in chili, meat loaf etc. with ground firm tofu. Doing so decreases your fat content, adds proteins and vitamins which are not found in beef, and reduces the environmental impact of the meal. There is no downside to this dietary practice. Pound for pound tofu is much cheaper than meat. It also contains anti-oxidants that boost our immune system and fight off free radicals that cause aging. There are numerous resource books on the market. Don't hesitate to use them.

● Whenever possible choose free range meat. This is both ethical and environmental. The quality of a creature's life is important to Empowerists. Many farmers are rejecting modern trends of mass animal protein production in favour of more traditional animal farming. Animals should have the capability to roam around freely rather than be raised in factory-style warehouses. Free range allows them to graze, play, form relationships, copulate and breed more naturally. From an environmental perspective, small farms are managed in harmony with surrounding ecology.

● Choosing vegetable and fruit produce that is organically grown and pesticide-free is both healthy and environmentally friendly. They are undeniably more expensive but sometimes empowerment comes with a price. These dietary recommendations are simply suggestions and not mandatory requirements. Every individual will choose his/her own level. As you gradually adopt the lifestyle of Empowerism, ideas and concepts that seemed difficult (and maybe ridiculous) at first, will easily become habits.

● Recommended websites:

www.montereybayaquarium.org — gives updated information on fish species that are environmentally friendly for consumption.

www.globalfoodideas.com — provides vegetarian recipes from around the world.

"Waste not, Want not"

"North Americans are the most wasteful people on the face of the Earth. In Rome, people put out little over 680 grams (1.5 lbs.) of trash a day; in Nigeria, it's about 450 grams (1 lb.). In North America, every day, each person throws out almost 1800 grams (4 lbs.) of waste. Over the course of a year, that's almost a ton of garbage per person. A typical North American goes through and discards 7 kilograms (16 lbs.) of junk mail and 54 kilograms (120 lbs.) of newsprint each year. Each hour, we throw away more than 2.5 million non-returnable, non-recyclable plastic bottles. A 1989 marine conference held in Halifax estimated that five million plastic containers were thrown into the world's oceans every day" (Gordon). These statistics are staggering and indicative of a lifestyle that is unacceptable to Empowerists who must live their lives with the goal of reducing this horrific onslaught of garbage.

Until we came along, the ecosystem had developed ways to deal with the garbage generated by its inhabitants. Dung beetles rushed to collect feces, birds and small mammals cleaned up suppertime leftovers, and death catered dinner for maggots and flies. In fact, for a large part of our history, the ecosystem could deal with human trash too. Now the garbage that we produce at an unprecedented rate is spilling over the limits of the planet's finite capacity to absorb it.

We have created a world where time is money, and convenience is profitable. We put our babies in disposable diapers, enough of them each year to stretch to the moon and back seven times. Worldwide, one billion trees are cut down annually for those fluffy liners in disposables. Every hour of work saved by a disposable diaper translates into hundreds of years of waste. Modern life is a garbage maker's perpetual-motion machine. Every year 1.6 billion pens, two billion razors and blades, and 246.9 million scrap tires are discarded; and every three months, North Americans throw away enough aluminum to rebuild the entire U.S. commercial airline fleet. In the United States, more than half of the paper and glass produced and about one-third of the plastics are incorporated in items with a life span of under one year" (Gordon).

● **Recycle!** Every little effort has an impact. You must believe this because it is true. Whatever you discard must either be sent for recycling or composted. It can take as much as a month for a love-letter to decompose in a landfill. Two to five centuries for an aluminum can … a glass bottle or plastic container … no one even knows. Throwing away an aluminum can wastes as much energy as pouring out a half-filled litre of gasoline.

● **Share newspapers at work.** One newspaper per household is excessive waste. Or simply get your news off the Internet, television or radio. You can access almost any daily newspaper from any country via your computer. Every ton of recycled newsprint -about 2,000 daily papers- reduces the need to cut down 17 trees.

● **Cook only what you and your dependants can consume before it becomes inedible.** In conjunction with this, try to purchase groceries in small quantities and only when you need them. Frequent trips to the local grocer en route to work or home, rather than weekly ones to stock up, allows for more manageable food consumption.

● **Buy locally!** Produce that has traveled a great distance has burned more fossil fuels than locally grown items. (Supporting members of your community is beneficial for reasons other than just environmental ones.)

● **Walk, cycle, roller-blade, or run whenever possible.** Always remind yourself that doing so is a physical empowerment of the physical self and is not damaging to Mother Earth.

● **Find a way to give away re-useable clothing and other items to agencies that can distribute them to others who can benefit from them.** Have a garage sale. One person's garbage is another person's treasure. (If you give away the proceeds to charity, you empower the endeavour ten-fold both altruistically and environmentally.)

I am not advocating a minimalist lifestyle but a reduction in consumption and consumerism. If you want a fancy sports car and can afford to buy one, then do so, but appreciate its value to your life and be ultimately aware of its basic function — that it is simply a means of transportation rather than an item to be flaunted.

Consumerism

*"There's a rich man sleeping in a golden bed
... There's a skeleton choking on a crust of
bread ..."*   STING

It is a fundamental belief of Empowerists that our level of consumerism has to be reduced. Humans have turned "dominion" over nature into consumption, exploitation and desecration. In conjunction with the increase in our wealth, corporations conveniently invent and provide new devices and products that "must" be incorporated into our lifestyle lest we run the risk of being "incomplete". There is no end to the level of consumption one can reach. We can shop at home online, while the television blares an ad for a new product, and if you're a complete shopaholic, you could be ordering something via the phone.

Empowerists have the ability to deconstruct the media's message of over-consumption and buy only what they truly need at that moment in time. They refrain from impulse buying and "last minute sales". They plan their shopping list and quickly make a mental justification of its purchase.

Saving money in the bank is another terrific strategy. Wealth safely stored in the bank is money that is not being spent on products extracted from Mother Earth. Invested properly, these finances can grow and be used on environmentally friendly merchandise, which is traditionally more expensive, or on entertainment provided by nature.

The following statistics demonstrate the lunacy of present levels of wealth and potential consumption:

● The top one-fifth of the world's population earns over 75 times the bottom one-fifth!

● Assets of the world's richest 200 people are larger than the combined annual income of the poorest 1 billion people!

Knowledge is Power

*"No tool is more beneficial than intelligence. No
enemy is more harmful than ignorance."*

ABU ABDULLAH MUHAMMED AL-HARITHI AL-BAGHDADI

(10th century Iraqi scholar)

There can be no denying that knowledgeable people stand out
in a crowd. They have empowered themselves with information
about the state of the world around them, current events, cultural nuances, the arts etc. Empowerists must never knowingly
benefit from someone else's adversity. This is extremely difficult
because it is often hard to acquire information about all the
goods we purchase and services we solicit. Empowerists,
however, must strive to avoid buying products produced by
individuals who work in less than favourable conditions and
boycott corporations that break environmental protection laws
in order to increase their profit margin. At the same time, companies that make concerted efforts to be environmentally and
labour friendly should be commended and rewarded with your
patronage.

The battle for human rights is a tough one as followers of
many old-world religions have passively accepted the persecution and suffering of others on the basis of their sex or
birthright. Hinduism has subscribed to the caste system for centuries, a concept that Mahatma Gandhi, a Hindu himself, passionately preached against. New, fundamentally Islamic regimes
are twisting ancient writings to allow for the brutal treatment of
women. Buddhism too, teaches that all life is suffering, a concept
that does not actively allow for persecution of others but leads
to complacency when suffering is evident. Empowerism does
not suggest that disciples of these religions give up the religion

itself, but only the concepts which allow for the degradation of others. Every human life is precious, and must be treated fairly, regardless of gender, social status, physical appearance and sexual orientation. Empowerists must arm themselves with the knowledge to fight against all persecution of others.

The following suggestions are obvious strategies to empowerment via the absorption of information that must be revisited in the modern era.

1. **Read:** In the modern world, television and the Internet have relegated print media to the fringes of the information world. But the written word is still a force to be reckoned with. The book you are holding and the facts you are reading give testimony to this. Literature transcends time. Reading is a dramatic way to enhance one's knowledge base. *What* you read is of utmost importance of course.

Magazines and newspapers, (preferably shared by a large group or on the Internet) are crucial to Empowerists, as one must be up-to-date on current events in order to make informed decisions about daily life. Medical updates about modern scientific discoveries and nutritional advancements are key as well. Empowered individuals openly embrace them in order to remain healthy and extend their quality of life into old age.

Non-fiction books are a good reading option because they offer factual data on whatever subject you have chosen. If you have read a great book that you feel has empowered you, share it with others and encourage them to share titles with you. Your time is finite; use it wisely, especially when it comes to leisure.

Fiction, too, is extremely beneficial. Delving into a book transports you into another time, spatial reality, or a character's mind and in turn sharpens your imaginative powers. As a teacher for 12 years, I have witnessed a complete apathy, even disdain toward reading by many students. "Hyper-entertainment", such as computer video games and the Internet have diminished students' desire and capacity to imagine. They prefer to be passive participants, nourished by the cathode ray tube and L.C.D. monitors in front of them. Many of them would rather watch the "movie" version than experience the book for themselves.

2. **Television:** Having just criticized television in the above section it seems ironic that it be listed as the next medium of knowledge acquisition. However, carefully planned television viewing can be very empowering. It is a good source for obtaining one's daily news. Empowerism advocates expanding the dimensions of one's knowledge base by focusing on world news. (The B.B.C. news has a great reputation for aggressive journalism and widespread global coverage.) Use television to update yourself on the state of the environment. New technologies and strategies should be embraced in order for you to properly do your part. Nature, Health, Cooking, and Children's Educational shows all convey information that is potentially empowering. (Too often, however, parents use television as an electronic baby-sitter, and although this is understandable in the hectic modern era, quality educational programming must be the empowered choice.)

3. **Listen:** People who are empowered do not preach pompously. They listen to and learn from other people's ideas, cultural idiosyncrasies and life experiences. Learning from others is active, rather than passive. It is often first hand and invaluable. Why not learn from others' trials and errors? Absorb this knowledge like a sponge, and filter out what is not empowering.

4. Music: Music is as uplifting as it is empowering. Incorporate it into your life whenever possible. Instrumental music is good for the soul and rhythm of life. Music with lyrics tells of yet another life experience and personal ideology.

5. Internet: The internet can be used as it is an unprecedented tool for decentralized grass roots movements which use it as a medium for free information sharing, petitioning and networking.

6. Travel: (But leave no footprints)

> *" Human beings are more alike than unalike, and what is true anywhere is true everywhere, yet I encourage travel to as many destinations as possible for the sake of education as well as pleasure."*
>
> MAYA ANGELOU, Writer and Poet

If you can, visit other "communities" in the global village. Knowledge of other cultures and other peoples' living standards is highly empowering. One generally comes to appreciate what they have at home when they experience how others endure the hardships of life. This is not to say that residents of less-developed nations lead lives that are any less fulfilling. In fact, people with very little are often more content. They find happiness in their daily routines, relationships and meager possessions. They are empowered by what little they have. It is those who have too much who keep searching for substance to fill a self-created void.

After you have traveled, share your experience and what you have learned. Empower others; those who are already empowered will listen. Traveling properly relies on the oral tradition. Nothing can replace first hand information derived from someone who has recently been to a destination. Many popular travel guides offer web sites that allow recent travelers to provide updates of travel in a country whether it be about the political climate, safety, new accommodation, weather and much more. (If everyone traveled with his or her eyes truly open, racism, too, would slowly be eradicated.)

In keeping with the environmental element of being empowered when traveling, leave no footprints.
● Do not exploit the local population – the tourist industry already does that.
● Tip properly when services are rendered. Do not hesitate to over-tip if you can afford it, especially if your dollar is much stronger than the local currency.
● Do not exploit the natural resources; shoot the local wildlife with a camera only!
● Eat what is local and abundant; take only what you can finish.
● Empower the people whom you encounter on your journey whether it is with kindness, gifts or extreme gratitude for their hospitality.
● All-inclusive resorts offer a dilemma because they are owned by consortiums that siphon the profits out of the needy host countries. But the resorts themselves provide necessary jobs for the local population who would be poverty stricken without them. So, research your holiday carefully! Try to select a destination that is generous with its employees and operates environmentally by recycling the monstrous amounts of plastic drinking containers etc. (Empowered individuals should reuse their drinking cups while staying at the resort.)

Eco-tourism: the rise of tourism that focuses on ecological flora and fauna serves a two-fold purpose. First, it exposes people to the pressures that the modern world has put on the environment and fosters a love and appreciation for what little remains. Secondly, it provides crucial dollars for grass roots movements and environmental groups who are trying to preserve the precious beasts and habitats that are holding on for dear life. While engaging in Eco-tourism, Empowerists must choose tour operators who work in conjunction with the local peoples and in turn share a portion of their profit with them.

Teaching as a Vocation

"A teacher affects eternity. He [she] can never tell where his [her] influence stops."

HENRY BROOKS ADAMS

Empowerists are life-long learners and teachers. This does not necessarily mean that they choose teaching as a career but that they share their knowledge and experience willingly and without the expectation of getting something in return. Empowerists never force knowledge upon others. They should transfer it to willing participants and always encourage active learning, field questions and provide references or alternate sources of information when they are unsure of the correct answer.

Sharing accurate knowledge about the state of the environment and offering up possible solutions in which individuals can potentially remedy them, is crucial to Empowerism. The primary goal of this book is to spread the concepts within it, in order for Empowerism to become a movement rather than just a philosophy.

Humans are intrinsically good. If they are gently made aware of how easy it is to change basic living habits in order to minimize their negative impact on the environment, they will do so. Sharing your experience is crucial.

1. Buy a composter for someone and demonstrate how simple it is to operate. Outline the benefits the resulting composted material can have on their lawns and gardens.

2. Help your neighbours plant a tree.

3. Build them a bird feeder so that animals in the vicinity have other "restaurant" options over and above your own handouts.

4. Share meatless or "meat-reduced" recipes with others ... or share the meals themselves. Once people have actually tried the

food realize that there is no compromise to the flavour and variety of the diet, they will be more apt to embrace the options that vegetarianism provides. (Once again, share the facts of how incorporating items such as tofu into one's diet reduces the environmental impact of the meal. Provide them with data that explains the scientifically proven cancer fighting qualities of soy and other meat alternatives.)

5. **Lend someone else this book (or supply them with a copy).**

Pets

"The animals of the planet are in desperate peril ... without free animal life I believe we will lose the spiritual equivalent of oxygen."
ALICE WALKER, Novelist and Poet

It is widely accepted that pets can provide an outlet for stress and teach children the fundamentals of responsibility. However, the keeping and maintaining of a living creature should never be taken lightly. When choosing a pet there are numerous situations that Empowerists should take into consideration.

Living Quarters: The quality of an animal's life is directly related to its living space. People who own large pets should have ample room for the animal to roam around. Large dogs, for example, should never be kept in apartments or small houses, as they require spacious areas to run around, even if they are walked twice a day. Birds should be housed in large aviaries to allow for flight. Cats should not be de-clawed as it deprives them of an essential weapon of self-defense against other animals.

Exotic Pets: Animals that have not been traditionally domesticated or are not indigenous to a region should not be kept as pets. However, if an individual is truly adamant about incarcerating an exotic animal and is willing to care for it at any cost, then a great deal of research should be done first. Exotic pets should be acquired from an experienced breeder who has raised them in captivity and has definitive proof of the captive breeding line. This practice eliminates the possibility that you are participating in the horrific illegal exotic pet trade that is systematically forcing wild animals into extinction.

Endangered Species: It goes without saying that animals that are on the endangered species list and regulated by international treaties should never be kept as personal pets.

Assisting wild animals in your neighbourhood can also be empowering. Regularly placing food out for wild birds and local wildlife provides supplemental nutrition for creatures that have become disenfranchised by the urban expansion of the modern era. Keep in mind that once you begin this practice, these creatures will visit regularly and will soon come to rely on your handouts to augment their diet.

Competition

Healthy competition with other people is beneficial on many levels. Training for any form of competitive activity strengthens the body and mind while providing opportunities to set goals for yourself. Competition has always been a driving force in the evolutionary process. However, while our survival does not depend on it, competition can offer an exciting dimension to our daily lives on an aesthetic level. Empowerists should incorporate competitive activities into their lives that are both challenging, allow for fun and foster life-long friendships.

Thrill seeking

"We live in a wonderful world that is full of beauty, charm and adventure. There is no end to the adventures that we can have if only we seek them with our eyes open."

JAHAWARAL NEHRU

The adrenaline rush created by activities that are slightly dangerous can be empowering only if they are conducted under tightly controlled conditions. Every measure must be taken to minimize the risk, while maintaining the thrill of the event. Empowerists are always aware of the reality that death empowers no one, especially themselves. Choose activities that are well-established as being safe and only solicit reputable establishments with an exemplary track record. As many "extreme" sports are connected within natural environments, always ensure that there is no permanent destruction to surrounding habitats and that businesses conduct their practice harmoniously with the natural world. Activities such as scuba-diving, white water rafting, skiing, snowboarding, kayaking and rock-climbing are all generally safe and environmentally friendly as long as the participants are properly trained and they "leave no footprints". Motorized thrills, although highly exciting, burn fossil fuels and often leave permanent scars on the environment. Empowerists must weigh the pros and cons of all their thrill-seeking activities, especially when participating in highly dangerous sports.

CHAPTER THREE

Sense of Self

"Love is, above all, the gift of oneself."
Jean Anouilh, French Playwright

Since Empowerism derives its energy from within, it follows therefore that a strong and positive sense of self is essential. No individual is exempt from personal insecurities, and if they claim to be, then they are definitely overcompensating for one. Empowerists are comfortable conducting regular self-evaluations that update their emotional, physical and spiritual state, and if there is a need for improvement then they embrace it, address it and fix it. If it can't be fixed, however, they take ownership of it and adopt coping strategies.

Body Image

As inhabitants of the modern world, we are constantly bombarded with the media's version of the archetypal body and if this isn't enough, we are offered products and methods by which we can diet, sculpt and alter ourselves in order to achieve this form. Empowerists do not buy into this. As long as they strive to be healthy and live a lifestyle in harmony with their surroundings, their physical body shape is of no consequence.

Mental State

Mental fitness, however, is harder to achieve. The societal pressure to achieve and acquire success is chipping away at our ability to attain happiness. When communities were much smaller, people knew their neighbours. They trusted them to look after their property and lend a helping hand when required. Ironically, many of us have lost this sense of "tribal" support as we live isolated in an urban crowd. This lack of community support has created an unnecessary burden on our mental state. Empowerists seek out moral support from people they trust, whether in the workplace, recreational/leisure groups, or family and friends. They never try to handle difficult situations alone. If you feel a little mentally unstable then ego is cast aside and aid is accepted until normalcy is restored. This of course, is always reciprocated. Assistance is never denied to a community member in need. It follows, therefore, that Empowerists must set up situations in which their network of friends is constantly increased and maintained.

Health

"A body seriously out of equilibrium, either with itself or with its environment, perishes outright."
GEORGE SANTAYANA,
Spanish poet and philosopher

Your sense of self relies on your health. Good health empowers your spirituality, your career and all those who depend on you. Attaining and maintaining good health is a major goal of Empowerism.

In order to do this, set aside a "guaranteed" minimum of half an hour EVERYDAY for yourself. One hour would be ideal, but this is an unrealistic daily time frame for most individuals. Invigorate yourself during this period by regularly conducting one of the activities listed below. It does not have to occur at the same time everyday, but should occur everyday.

Suggestions:

1. **Exercise:** One of the greatest things one can do for the mind, body and spirit is to exercise. Choose an activity suited to your lifestyle, age and physical fitness level. Cardiovascular activities are perfect, especially those conducted outdoors where one can enjoy nature's beauty. Weight training is an ideal method in which to strengthen the body in order to enable your frame to manage and cope with the strains of daily life. (Always consult a doctor before embarking on a vigorous regiment).

2. **Learn** and practise one of the ancient physical arts like Yoga, or Tai Chi. These disciplines are tried, tested and true activities that have empowered humankind for centuries.

3. Read: As mentioned earlier, reading is an activity that is slowly being relegated to the fringes of modern society. Today we prefer to be "hyper-entertained" by movies, television, the Internet or video games and although these all have merits in their own right, they diminish the scope of our own imaginations. Nothing can transport, stimulate or inform the mind more than a good book. The knowledge obtained from a book is also empowering, hence reading **this** book is empowering on numerous levels.

4. Talk to a friend: Communication with a friend via the phone, Internet or in person is empowering for many reasons. Talking is cathartic and listening is passive. Friendships over a lifetime are a testament to our goodness.

5. Pray: Prayer as a means of increasing your spiritual health is an undeniable truth. Whether conducted alone or with others, prayer elevates us from the rigours of daily life.

6. Cook/Eat: Good health and good food go hand in hand. Taking time out of a busy day to cook a healthy meal is empowering on many levels. Good nutrition takes planning and some preparation time. Fast food on the other hand is as good as its promise. It has been designed to fill the gaps (and stomachs) of an accelerated lifestyle and although it is an integral source of food for many and can meet our dietary requirements successfully, it cannot replace the beauty of a home-cooked meal. Varying your nutritional intake provides the body with many essential vitamins. Eating your own creations enables you to be aware of **all** the ingredients involved, especially if you have dietary restrictions for health and/or moral reasons.

Involve your children in the cooking ritual. Doing so is not only a bonding experience but provides an opportunity for them to learn about proper nutrition, environmentally friendly waste disposal, as well as a respect for food sources. Explore ethnic cooking for nutritional diversity and the pure pleasure of it. Focus especially on cooking styles that revolve around vegetarian dishes and use legumes and soy as an alternative to meat for sources of protein. (It is important to note here that cooking, as a household chore for yourself or your dependents, **does not fulfill** the half-hour requirement of personal downtime empowerment).

7. Intimacy: One of the best ways to increase both physical and emotional health is to spend some quality time being intimate with a significant other. Spend time conversing. Learn the art of massage together. Bathe each other. Make love to each other.

8. Learn a musical instrument: Learning to play an instrument is both exhilarating and empowering. It is a fantastic way to spend your half-hour as you can track your progress, not to mention that you'll probably have some time alone during the initial learning stages.

It must be reiterated that this empowering half-hour should be self-indulgent. Excise any feeling of guilt that this is selfish. Remember that you cannot look after your loved ones, friends, dependents, colleagues and career if **your** physical and mental health is not maintained. Do not rationalize that job-related activities, housework or family-related obligations would fulfill this half-hour. You still potentially have fifteen and a half waking hours to meet the needs of everyone else.

Sexual Intimacy

"It was the most fun I had without laughing."
WOODY ALLEN, referring to sex.
ANNIE HALL 1977

Your sexuality is truly a gift. Its exploration, enhancement and development can be very empowering. Embrace it. Bask in it when possible. Set up time before and after the act itself. Play games and make promises. Sex with a partner can only be empowering when both participants feel empowered by the moment.

1. **Monogamy** is definitely a partnership that sets up an environment for empowerment for both parties. It provides for long term communication and the understanding of each other's bodies and needs. Sex and monogamy have the potential for long term empowerment.

2. **Homosexuality:** No one should ever be judged because of his or her sexual orientation. Although this lifestyle is no longer underground, the "moral" majorities, especially those belonging to fundamental religious groups, still attach a stigma to this segment of society. Homosexuality has long been considered an "unnatural" expression of sexuality, but recent studies on animal populations have discovered widespread male-on-male and female-on-female sexual activity. Researchers believe the practice diffuses tensions and creates alliances amongst animals groups. In any case, humans have long since lost the ability to define what is natural versus unnatural. The urban jungles in which we live, the cars and planes in which we travel around, and even the food we ingest, are a far cry from the "natural" state that

we evolved in. Empowerists understand that any expression of sexual intimacy, as long as all the participants are consenting adults, is acceptable behaviour.

3. Masturbation: Self-gratification has been a taboo for most religions and cultures for far too long. It is completely absurd for this attitude to continue as virtually all medical studies from the 60's onward have discovered physical and mental benefits of masturbation. It is practical, safe sex in a potentially dangerous environment. Empowered individuals are aware of their bodies, meet the needs of their sexual self and feel absolutely no guilt about it.

Happiness

"If we imagine that the fullness we yearn for can be reckoned in dollars ... or purchased in stores, there will be no end to our craving."

DAVID SUZUKI

Happiness is a state of mind. We expend the same amount of energy being in a good mood as being in a bad mood, except a good mood is highly contagious. For some reason what used to make people happy has been lost. In this modern age we are told from day one that success is determined by our possessions. We educate ourselves and then choose a career that will provide enough money to buy all the things that we are told we need. But ultimately whoever dies with the most stuff ... still dies.

So what creates happiness? On a scientific level, feelings of euphoria are created by bursts of dopamine and/or seratonin created by the body when it is positively stimulated. Events like sports activities, falling in love, sexual intimacy, a good meal and a sense of accomplishment all trigger a release of these natural chemicals produced by the human body. Almost all of these activities involve another individual and can be done at little or no cost. In light of this, Empowerists must choose activities that make them happy and create a strong feeling of self-worth in themselves and in others around them.

Grief

"Between grief and nothing ... I will take grief."
William Faulkner

As the resources of the earth are finite, so too are human lives. Undoubtedly, in our lifetime we will experience the pain of the loss of a loved one or the knowledge of your own impending demise. The resulting grief is proof that you exist and that there is indeed a self. In order for the grief to be dealt with, the grief must be embraced. The pain you feel is real. It defines you at that moment. Surround yourself with friends. Discuss it. Share it. Others who are empowered will be there for you. If there is truly no one around to help, then use this experience to empower yourself further in order to support others in their moments of grief.

Loss of a Loved One

You are grieving because you have lost someone you loved. At these times, it is important to focus on why you loved them. What did they do to empower your life?

> Reflect on it. Meditate on it. Cherish it. Share it.
> Pay homage to them because they deserve it.
> Whatever they did to make you love them, do to others around you.

Empower yourself and others the way the deceased empowered you. In this way, too, their legacy will live on.

Tragic loss

By far, the hardest time to believe or harness any power from within or above is during a tragic or unexpected loss. You will question and challenge your level of empowerment, but by focusing on the belief that you will eventually triumph, the tragedy will be transcended.

1. Grieve. It is your right.
2. Immediately draw upon support and strength from others. Being alone during a tragic loss is not empowering.
3. Do not question God. No answers will be provided.
4. Do not be angry with God or others. This is energy that could be spent empowering yourself.

Your level of empowerment is never static. A simple goal of Empowerism is to maintain your level of empowerment in the hope of increasing it. There will be moments in your life that will create the ILLUSION that your empowerment has been shattered. Although this may seem real, depending on the tragedy, a truly empowered individual will understand that every situation can be dealt with and solved over time and with the support of others.

Addiction

"Every form of addiction is bad no matter whether the narcotic be alcohol, morphine or idealism." Carl Jung

It goes without saying that empowerment is impossible if your life is plagued by an addiction. But Empowerism and recovery can go hand in hand. The first step is simple. You must declare yourself a proponent of Empowerism and subscribe to its philosophy and lifestyle amendments. Overcoming the addiction, of course, is the difficult part. Modern society is a breeding ground for addictions, whether they involve nicotine, alcohol, gambling or hard drugs. We are pressured by the media to eat more, drink more, buy more merchandise, play the lottery, etc. We are brainwashed into believing that by doing so we will fill the voids in our lives.

Empowered individuals can elevate themselves from all of this and realize that self-worth comes from within. Eating, drinking and shopping are all necessary for our daily lives but we must limit the intake to what we truly need. At its basic level, addiction is submitting control to a substance or repetitive, destructive action (gambling, shopping, etc.). Once an individual is empowered, control over one's life is inevitable. For the few extreme cases, such as those individuals whose recovery is complicated by histories of hereditary addiction, strong physical attachment to highly addictive substances, and addiction linked to depression, a declaration of empowerment must be made and immediate professional help sought. Engage all the assistance possible from family, friends, former addicts, resource books and addiction agencies as well as other available support groups/networks.

When the addiction is realized, treated and conquered, Empowerism will be the key to avoiding relapse. Every moment that a recovered individual remains empowered is time spent in positive territory. Whether it be exercising, gaining knowledge, volunteering somewhere where your talents are needed or planning the next vegetarian meal, your life will be productive rather than destructive.

CHAPTER FOUR

Money

There is no doubt that in the 21st Century, money is power. But we spend far too much time wishing for more of it when time could be spent becoming empowered with the money we have at the moment. The following strategies should be employed in order to increase the power of your present financial status and ensure that provisions are made for your future.

1. Demand proper value for what you purchase or for the services you contract, without being aggressive or obnoxious.

2. Reject the media's brainwashing that your self-worth is determined by your possessions. Buy only what you truly need.

3. If you cannot afford it, stop wanting it and derive satisfaction from the items you presently have.

4. There are numerous ways to entertain yourself cheaply. Exercise, meditate, volunteer, etc.

5. Buy life insurance. Any financial planner will tell you that life insurance is a sound method of ensuring that your partner or dependants are looked after financially at the time of your death (especially if it is sudden). Like all financial planning, money grows over time. Therefore, a policy will be much cheaper if purchased at a young age because the money invested will appreciate during your lifetime. Smart parents buy policies on their children. Although this appears morbid, it is very strategic. The policy exists for the life span of the child, so in essence you are providing for your grandchildren. In the tragic event that your child should die, the policy will be a financial legacy that can be used to empower the lives of the rest of your family or for an altruistic cause of your choice, (an environmental protection or wildlife conservation group perhaps).

6. Invest wisely. If you are in the lucrative position of being able to put money away for your future, then research carefully and invest cautiously. Paying a professional money manager is intelligent (tips from friends "in the know" are seldom worth while in the long run).

7. Only play the stock market with money you can absolutely, positively afford to lose! Over the last few decades, countless stories have been told of how individuals turned their meager savings into fortunes. Empowerists understand that for every lucky investor there is an unbalanced proportion of bankrupt individuals. (Make an effort to invest in environmentally friendly companies.)

Altruism

"Don't give till it hurts. Just Give!"

CHRISTOPHER MARK D'SOUZA

Ignore anyone that tells you that no act is truly altruistic. By being altruistic you empower someone else. If it makes you feel good by doing it, you double its altruistic value. Empowerists must live their lives with the understanding they must perform altruistic acts whenever possible. And after the task has been conducted, revel in it. Feel good about yourself.

In order to facilitate this altruistic lifestyle, contribute to or become members of any of the following groups:

Amnesty International
Greenpeace
P.E.T.A – People for the Ethical Treatment of Animals
Free the Children
World Wildlife Federation
The Audubon Society
World Vision
Doctors Without Borders
The National Geographic Society
The Jane Goodall Society
The Digit Foundation (Diane Fossey's Mountain Gorilla
    legacy)
The David Suzuki Foundation

Altruism: unselfish devotion to the welfare of others

CHAPTER FIVE

Actions Speak Louder

Politically Correct Language

Using language that is offensive to another individual is empowering to no one. It demonstrates a complete lack of sensitivity on the part of the speaker and creates negative emotions. On the other hand, using inclusive and politically correct language portrays an intelligent and compassionate personality that is empowered and willing to empower others. Keeping abreast of current and updated politically correct terminology is not an easy task, but will get easier when one begins to network with other Empowerists.

Compliment/Praise Others

Recognizing someone's accomplishments is extremely empowering. Just think back to the last time someone complimented you on your appearance, or thanked you for something you did. Words cost nothing. Give them away. Make it a point to empower others on a daily basis by praising and complimenting them for even little tasks or achievements. Do so especially if someone has done something to make your day easier.

Hypocrisy

"Hypocrisy is the most difficult and nerve-racking vice that any [hu]man can pursue; it needs an unceasing vigilance and a rare detachment of spirit. It cannot, like adultery or gluttony, be practised at spare moments; it is a whole-time job."

SOMERSET MAUGHAM

Hypocrisy is rampant in the third millenium. Too many people are far too comfortable saying one thing and doing another. They profess a devotion to a religion, secretly disobey many of the fundamental laws, and then are racked with guilt. To make matters worse, the media glorify people who abuse their positions of power and often give them a forum for their immoral views and behaviour.

The fundamental concepts of Empowerism are easy to follow and, therefore, the capacity for Empowerists to be hypocritical is diminished. Living amongst hypocrites is a more difficult task. Unfortunately, we must co-exist with such individuals in the workplace, at school and in our communities. Avoid hypocrites whenever possible and make a gentle effort to change those close to you if you think there is a chance of success.

Humour

"Humour is perhaps a sense of intellectual perspective: an awareness that some things are really important, others not; and that the two kinds are most oddly jumbled in everyday affairs."

CHRISTOPHER MORLEY

A sense of humour and laughter are truly underrated gifts from God. Many moments in our life have an untapped potential for humour. Empowerism suggests that we harness this potential and use it when it is practical and appropriate. Laughter is spiritually invigorating, as long as it does not occur at the expense of someone else.

Passion

"Passion is universal humanity. Without it religion, history, romance and art would be useless."

HONORÉ DE BALZAC

If apathy is one of the major diseases of the modern era, then passion is a possible cure. Becoming passionate about something, whether it is a cause, a person, a goal or even a hobby, can fuel a zest for life. If it is something you enjoy then it is empowering. Sharing that passion with someone you feel passionate about is exponentially empowering.

Respect for Others

Racism

"Sometimes, it's like a hair across your cheek. You can't see it, you can't find it with your fingers, but you keep brushing at it because the feel of it is irritating."

MARIAN ANDERSON

Scientific discoveries by the Human Genome Project have proven that the basic building blocks of the human body differ very little from each other. Over time, human physical features have evolved in many different and beautiful ways in order to adapt to a complex array of environments. But humans are one species. It goes without saying, therefore, that for Empowerists, racism is ludicrous! No individual should ever be persecuted, judged or discriminated against based on his/her racial background. In fact, Empowerism dictates that its followers actively work toward racial harmony. Racial differences should be embraced, shared and exhalted. Racial pride should be fostered in conjunction with a desire to learn as much as possible about other cultures, customs, etc. Racism is a negative by-product of ignorance. Knowledge is power. Gaining wisdom about the wonderful diversity that permeates humankind is extremely empowering. Networking and making life-long friends with people of other races is divine.

There are three basic types of racism: **1.** Systemic; **2.** Overt; **3.** Subliminal.

1. Systemic Racism is racism that is written and enforced by governmental or institutional policy. Although it is rare in the third millenium, there are still governments in the world that implement and actively protect policies that persecute groups and individuals based on race.

2. Overt Racism is any blatant verbal or physical attack carried out against an individual or group based on race by an individual or group. Hate crimes perpetuated by white supremacist groups fall under this category.

3. Subliminal Racism is by far the most dangerous and most rampant. These individuals claim to be tolerant and even respectful of other races but unknowingly judge others based on race. (I would much rather be confronted by an overt racist because I am aware of my persecutor … subliminal racism affects my daily activities and is difficult to combat.)

Human Rights

"All human beings are born free and equal in dignity and rights."
UNIVERSAL DECLARATION OF HUMAN RIGHTS

Human Rights issues should be prevalent in the minds of Empowerists. Many of the freedoms that we enjoy in the modern era such as freedom from oppression, freedom of speech, religion and assembly are denied to populations around the world. There are many ways to fight against this injustice such as writing letters, lobbying governments and joining established human rights groups such as Amnesty International. (Refer back to Altruism)

Judging others

The Christian Bible quotes Christ as having said, "Let he [or she] who is without sin, cast the first stone." North American Aboriginal folklore suggests that we should, "never judge another unless you have walked a mile in their moccasins." Both doctrines offer up the same message: that no person is ever in a position to judge another. Empowerists, too, subscribe to this message and incorporate it into their daily lives.

Ironically, fundamental Christian groups (along with fundamental Islamic religions) openly preach against homosexuality and feminism. It makes no sense really. Humans should be allowed to live their lives, (as long as they do not infringe on the rights of others) in a manner that they choose, regardless of gender, age, sexual preference, skin colour, size, religion, physical challenges and philosophy.

The Elderly

"There was no respect for youth when I was young, and now that I am old, there is no respect for age — I missed it coming and going."

J. B. PRIESTLY

Up until the 1960's the term "elder" referred to a wise and respected individual. The elderly were esteemed members of society, whether they were productive or not, because their knowledge and experience were valued by those younger than themselves. Fast-paced technological advancements of the modern era, however, now make things obsolete on a yearly, if not monthly, basis. Older people have found it increasingly difficult to keep up with this pace and have been slowly relegated to the fringes of society. They rely on the much younger population to keep them up to date with new technology and gadgets that people used to do without. Younger generations though, have little or no time to share their knowledge with those who paved the way for their comfortable existence. As the population gets older, the struggle to provide a quality way of life for the elderly has gotten more complicated. The "old ways" no longer exist in many urban and even rural areas of the modern world. Empowerists must strive to bridge this ever-increasing gap between the old and the modern.

The elderly, too, must be empowered. Health permitting, they should learn or be taught how to use the modern devices that have become commonplace in the new millenium. Empowered teenagers should volunteer in Senior Citizen homes and assist the elderly onto the information super-highway. The results could be astonishing. Some of these people have survived the great wars, witnessed the introduction of cars, telephones, computers, and the threat of nuclear annihilation; finding their way around a VCR, cell phone or hand-held computer could be a breeze.

Much of the content of this book is not foreign to the elderly members of our society, as it contains concepts that they have been aware of for a long time. Conversing with them, basking in their knowledge and letting them know that their wisdom is appreciated is empowering for everyone involved (of course it must be said that the aged are as diverse as any population and contain racists, hypocrites and individuals who care little for the environment … these individuals should be taught the error of their ways or be given a wide berth.)

Role Models

"Think of the poorest person you have ever seen and ask yourself if your next act will be of any use to him [or her]."

MAHATMA GANDHI, (EPITAPH)

Choosing and following the path of a real person whom you respect is empowering on many levels. Firstly, a good role model provides tangible proof that success and happiness are truly attainable and that goal setting can be profitable. These individuals are often a great source of inspiration and wisdom because of their positive lifestyle. Good role models are often people who co-exist with us, and are no more super-human than ourselves. Teachers, parents, grandparents, employers and even neighbours are all potentially good candidates. Others are historical figures such as Gandhi who lived by the words he professed. His philosophy of passive resistance, used successfully by Martin Luther King Jr. two decades later, has faded into oblivion. Children of the third millennium need to be reminded of Gandhi's ideology and the success it has had for humankind.

Heroes

*"Without heroes we are all plain people and
don't know how far we can go."*
BERNARD MALAMUD

Heroes, too, can be inspirational. Unlike role models, they are
often people who are larger than life, sometimes historical
giants, who have become superstars because of their massive
achievements and resulting media attention. Empowerists
understand however, that no matter how famous a person is,
they are still human. Researching biographical material and
incorporating strategies used by your heroes to become "heroic"
can be empowering. One's heroes do not have to be superstars,
of course. It is quite common and endearing that a humble
person in one's life is revered as heroic.

Blame

Blame empowers no one. In fact, it contributes to the apathy that is rampant in the modern era. If everyone took responsibility for his or her own actions, the world would be a much better place. It is too easy to blame past generations for the dismal state of the environment and then justify complacency because it is not "our" problem. It is becoming increasingly obvious, however, that attitudes have got to change or the earth will die beneath our feet. Large corporations need to pay for the traditionally free resources the earth has provided rather than skirt environmental protection laws.

Empowerists must live their lives de-constructing blame. Energy that you would previously waste blaming others should be re-directed and channeled into solving immediate problems and ensuring that they do not happen again.

Regret

"Remorse causes cancer of the soul."
JOHN IRVING, *THE CIDER HOUSE RULES*

Regretting the actions of your past is a waste of energy that could be spent taking stock of one's accomplishments. If this is hard to do, then simply compliment yourself for having chosen to become an Empowerist, because there are only great things in store for you. Remember that Empowerism's goal is to eradicate negativity and to make the individual aware of how simple it is to become a truly beautiful entity.

Forgiveness

"To err is human; to forgive divine."
ALEXANDER POPE

The ability to forgive is a demonstration of a strong sense of self and a high level of maturity. It recognizes the fallibility of human nature and a willingness to move forward in your life. Dwelling on the negative actions of others toward you is a waste of time and energy. Depending on the severity of the act, Empowerists must strive to engage the other party in constructive dialogue and rectify the situation as soon as possible. Forgiveness has to be absolute; there can be no residue of animosity toward the individual, especially since human nature allows animosity to fester with the potential to re-surface later on in relationships.

At the same time, Empowerism dictates that if you are the wrongdoer, every effort must be made so that forgiveness is bestowed upon you. If reconciliation is impossible, extricate the person from your life and move on. Focus on the people around you who have a history of empowering you and vice versa. The only thing you should retain is the lessons learned from your own mistakes and the willingness to make a conscious effort to avoid repeating the same situation in the future.

CHAPTER SIX

Relationships

I have chosen to write this chapter in the first person because relationships is a complex subject to summarize in a ninety page book on lifestyle and environmental ethics and I found that this narrative simplified my task. Every moment of our lives takes place within the confines of a relationship. Whether it be with oneself, family, friends, significant other and most importantly Mother Earth, relationships provide a frame of reference and make us whole.

Since every person is unique, it follows that every relationship is infinitely complex and that no amount of rules or doctrines can address every one of them properly. From my short time here on earth however, this is what I have learned, and profoundly believe is sound advice on relationships:

Your partner in life, whether its is a long-term friend, spouse, boyfriend or girlfriend or significant other, should be your ultimate priority. His/her needs and desires must be put in front of yours. In order for the relationship to be successful however, the other party in the relationship must subscribe to the same precept. *You* must be *his/her* ultimate priority.

Parenting

"Children are the only form of immortality that we can be sure of."

PETER USTINOV

Our children are our legacy. Aside from carrying our genetic code they are a testament to our morality, ideology and spirituality. There is no doubt that parenting in the modern era has become highly complex. Many influences that shape our kids did not exist twenty years ago, such as the Internet, video games, cell phones and over 500 television stations. So how does a parent combat these distractions while still providing the positive conveniences these technological gadgets offer? The key is to instill a strong sense of self-respect and responsibility while maintaining constant lines of communication with your children. If a child knows that a parent is always accessible and approachable then a solution to every situation and dilemma can be found. The empowered parent will forge a friendship with their child while maintaining a hierarchy so that disciplinary measures can be enforced when necessary. Spending quality time is the only sure-fire method of forming this relationship and keeping it strong throughout the formative and adolescent years.

Parenthood should be planned for a number of reasons. In order for the experience to be completely empowering, children should not be brought into a situation of emotional or financial distress (doing so potentially compromises your environmentally friendly lifestyle). Raising a child comes with immense responsibilities, therefore, proper planning ensures that you have the financial means to raise the child in a manner that emotionally, physically and spiritually nurtures them. Empowerists who are parents must continue to live a lifestyle

that is non-disruptive to the environment by setting up strategies to avoid disposable diapers and other environmental
stresses whenever possible.

Having children must be a conscious and mature decision
because every new individual is potentially harmful or helpful
to the planet depending on how they live their life. "Consider
this: more people have been added to the Earth during the past
40 or 50 years than have been added since the dawn of man"
(Gordon). The world's population is growing by three people
every second. The 1990's saw faster increases in human numbers
than any other decade in history. Over the next 10 years the 6
billion people we have now will increase by over a billion. That's
like adding another China to the planet. Dire projections come
from the Washington-based Population Crisis Committee, a
leading U. S. organization that monitors population growth.
They predict that if present birth and death rates continue, we
will be struggling to accommodate almost 11 billion people on
Earth within the next 30 years. And that will continue in a dis-
astrous upward spiral to 27 billion by the end of the next
century. Most of those new mouths to feed will be born to
impoverished Third World families who barely subsist now.

To place all of that into perspective, just look at the next 30
years, says Robert Ornstein. It means that it took 10,000 human
lifetimes for us to grow to two billion, and in the course of one
human lifetime, we are going from two billion to ten billion.
The impact that each one of those billions has on the global
environment is magnified by technologies like automobiles and
the burning of coal and chemicals like CFCs and hundreds of
thousands of other chemicals that are doing serious damage.
Those are the concerns that grow daily with every new person
added to our numbers. Too many people equals too much pollution, too much destruction of the natural habitat and the

Earth's life-support systems. The fear is that the rise will happen so fast and be so steep that the world's resources will quickly run out. Complicating the whole issue is the fact that a child born in the West consumes 90 per cent more of the earth's natural resources than a child born in the Third World. (Gordon)

Empowerist parents must instill in their children a respect for nature and the environment and an appreciation for all that is provided for them. Parents should not deprive their children of the luxuries of a Western lifestyle, but should provide items that are both entertaining, instructional and not simply the objects of some monthly fad.

In the child's early years, entertainment and excursions should take place in the natural world — swimming, hiking, camping, scuba diving etc. — let nature be their theme park. But if they have their hearts set on a Disney style excursion, ensure that they are properly educated about the event in which they are being indulged and keep the excesses to a minimum.

Adolescence

"You don't have to suffer to be a poet; adolescence is enough suffering for everyone."

JOHN CIARDI

Adolescence is by far the most difficult time of our lives. It is during this period that we are taught (or forced) to be more responsible while we undergo excruciating physical changes which constantly undermine our egos. Pressure from adolescent peers is often a more powerful force than parental nurturing and is sometimes destructive if not handled with maturity.

Empowerism can be a positive influence on two levels:

1. Empowerists need to do everything they can to make the transition from childhood to adolescence and into adulthood as empowering as possible. Teenagers need to be nurtured, encouraged, supported and monitored on a constant basis. Their fears need to be quelled, their questions addressed, their maturing process accommodated and their opinions listened to. Think back to your adolescence. What knowledge do you possess now that would have made life easier for you then? Share it with an adolescent. They are impressionable. Empower them before they choose a path that is destructive to themselves and the world in which they live.

2. Adolescents need to take an active role in empowering themselves. Whether it be simply joining the Empowerist movement or affiliating themselves with people or groups that will empower them, the goal is the same: to steer away from activities that are psychologically, physically, emotionally and spiritually destructive to themselves and to abstain from actions that are environmentally damaging.

CHAPTER SEVEN

Empowered People

1. **Protect the environment.**
2. **Ask questions** (whoever asks a question looks foolish for a brief moment, but if the question is never asked then they remain a fool forever.)
3. **Are not afraid to speak publicly.**
4. **Smile at strangers.**
5. **Share their empowerment.**
6. **Try ... ... try again.**
7. **Sometimes fail like everybody else,** but learn from their mistakes, do more research and try again (or simply move on to something more productive).
8. **Take stock of their shortcomings,** rectify them or compensate for them by emphasizing and focusing on their strengths.
9. **Are patient.**
10. **Plan ahead.**
11. **Believe in themselves.**
12. **Compliment others** (verbally and spatially).
13. **Make eye contact while conversing.**
14. **Are rarely heard cursing.**
15. **Are never rude.**
16. **Empathize sincerely.**
17. **Are understood clearly.**
18. **Sympathize dearly.**
19. **Keep journals of reflection.**
20. **Can handle rejection.**
21. **Respect their elders.**
22. **Question their own motives.**
23. **Are cautious.**
24. **Respect and protect Nature.**

PART II

How I Became Empowered

The purpose of this section of the book is twofold. First and foremost, I want to demonstrate how humble and similar much of my life experience has been compared to most peoples', and in doing so let you make the connection that **Empowerism** is attainable for everyone at any stage of their life. Secondly, I hope that sharing a few facts about myself will validate that this philosophy is a result of life experiences, not simply something I read from a book, paraphrased and then regurgitated. The following discourse is not required reading on the road to empowerment, but I hope that it will create a bond between you and myself, and ultimately be empowering for both of us.

Growing Up

I was not born with a silver spoon in my mouth. My parents were hard working immigrants who traveled to the West in search of a better life for the family they were about to have. My father was born in Bombay, India to a family that was Catholicized by the Portuguese. Culturally, his ancestors intermarried with the Portuguese colonialists and integrated both their language and religious customs. He married my mother who was also born in India but had Spanish, British and Indian grandparents. They traveled to Canada in 1964 on an Indian Ship owned by a company for whom my father had worked as a radio-operator for eighteen years. My mother was five months pregnant at the time and concealed this from Canadian authorities for fear of losing their landed immigrant status. She was a qualified teacher but could not work in her condition. My dad was thirty-five and my mother was twenty-seven at the time. They had two hundred dollars between them and after spending over six weeks traveling by sea, (as the shipping company my dad had just retired from gave him free passage), they arrived in Canada. My dad washed dishes while they bunked with my mom's sister. I was born on November 14th of that year on a cold winter's day, (I still dislike the cold), and the family immediately migrated to Nakina, north of Lake Superior and the northern-most town accessible by road. My dad took on a job there as a radio operator for the Canadian government.

My sister was born eleven months after I was, and the completed family settled in a quiet Toronto suburb a few years later. My father continued to work for the Ministry of Transportation at the federal level until he retired at the age of sixty-five. His job took him away from home for about two weeks of every month, as he had to travel around the province of Ontario inspecting the instrument landing systems of all the provincial airports. He worked hard at his career, took pride in his work and when he retired at the age of 65 he was the project manager of his department. He instilled in me a strong work ethic and impressed upon me that because I was coloured in a "white" world, I had to look respectable at all times and achieve twice as much in order to be successful.

As the youngest of eight children, my dad's parents were old when he finally became a father, so he and my mother saved tirelessly in order to raise enough money to return to India. The goal was for me to meet my grandparents before they died. My father was the only child to leave India in search of a better life and he was determined to return to prove that his decision was a good one. But my grandmother died in 1969 and two months before my family arrived in India in the summer of 1970, my grandfather passed on as well. My father was heartbroken. I was the only grandchild out of 21 that carried the name Mark, after my grandfather … and he never lived to meet his namesake.

My mother returned to teaching shortly after my sister was born, as the family needed her income in order to make ends meet. She managed house and home while working full time and did double-duty when my dad was out of town. She scrutinized my schoolwork meticulously to ensure that I would be academically successful. From the day I was born, my parents made it known that there was no other option but to go to university.

On top of her regular motherly duties, my mother opened the doors of our home to anyone who was in need. Numerous family members who immigrated to Canada resided with us until they got their bearings and could forge out on their own. To this day she "incubates" newcomers and gently eases them out of the nest, armed with all they will need to be healthy, happy and safe. There is no doubt in my mind that much of my empowerment comes from these two resourceful and caring individuals who left a large family support system in India, ventured out on their own, and set up shop half way around the world in a foreign country.

My parents worked hard at their careers while trying to provide my sister and me with the basic amenities of life. We took camping holidays during summers and were treated with a trip to India almost every seven years as my parents still had strong family ties to their birthplace and wanted to instill a strong cultural pride in their children. During these trips to India I formed strong bonds with my first cousins and although they lived in the upper middle class of this third world nation, their standard of living was nothing compared to that of the West. I began to appreciate the comforts and luxuries of my Canadian homeland even though my family lived humbly. I never again took for granted the ability to drink water straight from the tap and I would constantly admire the vast array of entertainment and opportunities that were afforded me.

"White-wished"

Growing up coloured in a white world had its drawbacks though. I was often the only visible minority in my class and I developed strong insecurities about my appearance and sense of self largely due to the fact that I looked so different. In grade three the teacher was extremely strict and although I was meek and studious, she often found fault with my behaviour and belittled me in class. I began to dread going to school and my fear manifested itself in real health disorders. My dad addressed the situation with a concerned letter and her attitude altered enough for me to finish the year, broken and lacking all self esteem. Looking back, I guess she must have been a subliminal racist. I hope she changed her attitude or left the profession.

High school contributed to an even greater array of neurosis. Adolescence is traumatic enough for the normal teen; I had the added "curse" of being one of only five visible minorities in a school of over fifteen hundred students. I spent the first three years of my high school career being "white-wished". I downplayed my heritage as much as possible and hid behind a persona that was highly non-confrontational and drew little attention to myself. I retreated home soon after the bell rang and focused on learning the piano and guitar. I was horrible at sports too, as I was terribly lanky and prone to injury. This added to my level of insecurity as playing on a school team would have afforded me some much needed attention from my peers.

Everything began to change for the better when I turned seventeen. I attribute this to **two** significant events: Firstly, my dad forced me to get a job to earn a little pocket money and gain some desperately needed independence (my father was blatantly aware of my shy personality and anemic physical stature and was secretly worried about me.) So I got a job as a bus-boy at a local up-scale eatery. I lasted seven and half-hours before quitting, but I did so for good reasons. Unloading the dishes from the massive industrial dishwasher burned my hands, but more importantly I made the observation that everyone around me in the dungeon of the restaurant was coloured, while the waiters and hostesses, who had access to tips, were white. This disparity seemed unfair to me and I wanted no part of it, so I told the boss I was quitting but not before I got my hard earned thirty-five dollars. When I got home and told my dad I had quit, he was devastated. But when I explained my reasons he slowly came to terms with it and might have even gained a little respect for his 110-pound-weakling of a son.

I turned this failure into a positive opportunity. I knew that my many years of piano lessons had provided me with a talent that parents wanted for their children for which they were willing to pay. So I put up an advertisement in the local supermarket announcing that I would teach piano to beginner students, and I would do so in their own homes. Many hours in the waiting rooms of my piano teachers taught me that parents resented having to deliver their kids door to door for music lessons (they didn't mind screaming in a freezing hockey arena at their athletically gifted children, but music lessons always seemed to be a necessary chore). So I exploited this aspect of parenthood and one year later I had sixteen students in a five-mile radius at ten dollars an hour, while my friends were slogging for six. I made my own hours and was my own boss. I related well to my students and enjoyed struggling with them through their lessons. Because of my success, I was soon being referred to parents who had already enrolled their kids in music schools. Word had spread that I augmented my lessons with jazz, blues and pop styles that appealed to the kids as they quickly got bored with a strictly classical curriculum. When I finally got my driver's license, I had a roster of 25 students, five of whom were adults who were really eager to learn contemporary music and a waiting list of about 15 families. I continued to teach music for the next 20 years. It empowered me financially and intellectually, as I was forced to keep my musical skills sharp and make sure the lessons were challenging for my students. By the time I stopped teaching music, I was providing instructions for the piano, guitar and drums and had taught close to two hundred students.

Later on, in the same year that I began my roving music school, I also fell in love; as deeply in love as any seventeen-year-old boy could be. She was a blond-haired, blue-eyed girl whom I was convinced knew nothing of my existence. But we slowly became good friends and dated off and on for over two years. It was a turbulent relationship as she bounced back and forth between myself and her previous boyfriend whose father was dying. I believe that at the time she was truly infatuated with me but felt a great deal of guilt about leaving her ex-boyfriend at a difficult time in his life. What she brought to my life was invaluable. By loving me, she made me realize that I had a great deal of self-worth. The relationship, though excruciating, did wonders for my self-esteem. I broke out of my cocoon and began to experience life and all of its mysterious wonders.

In my final year of high school, on a dare, I auditioned for the school musical production, a 'rock-opera' and got the lead role! The experience was beyond fantastic. We rehearsed for three months, five days a week and performed to a packed house for three nights. I actually sang in front of a live audience. I felt like there was nothing I couldn't do (I was actually kicked out of all the dancing scenes by the director because of my horrible co-ordination but that minute setback did not phase me in the least). More importantly, I realized that there was no valid reason for me to be insecure about myself. If people laughed at me, then hopefully I had brightened up their day and, if they judged me, their assumptions could not affect my life. I had become empowered but was not really aware of it at the time.

I finished high school and returned to India for a fourth time to spend time re-connecting with the cousins I had met seven years before. I spent two months traveling the magnificent countryside only to return for another four months immediately after my first year in university. Emotionally, I was getting more attached to this third world country rather than the country of my birth. I was amazed at how full people's lives were even though they possessed so little. They found happiness in family and friends and spent quality time nurturing relationships rather than chasing the almighty dollar.

I slowly began to lose my sense of self-identity. I no longer related to my friends at home as they had not shared in my cultural experiences of the last two years. Their goals seemed shallow and materialistic. I felt alone and isolated from everything I cared about. I even contemplated leaving university for a few years and spending the time in India. I felt loved there. The people there were real. But the idea was absurd and I slowly came to my senses and focused on my studies. I finished my degree with a major in English and a minor in Anthropology and as my marks were too low to get me into the Faculty of Education, I ended up pursuing a Masters in Environmental Studies. The year I spent in this program was intellectually exhausting while at the same time terrifying. Every day I was exposed to a new environmental crisis: C.F.Cs were deteriorating the ozone, fossil fuel emissions were contributing to global warming, destruction of rain-forests was a global epidemic and as Dr. Suzuki stated, "the increasing population would constantly be on a collision course with the life support systems of the earth" (not to mention the rapid extinction of precious animal species, pollution that was creating inhabitable regions of the earth and the A.I.D.S. epidemic). It was so overwhelming that I felt I was on the verge of a serious depression. The apathy and ignorance of the people around me regarding these issues compounded my emotional confusion. So in order to save myself, I left the program, one course short of a Master's degree. I was accepted into The Faculty of Education and jumped at the chance to bail on the "doom and gloom" of the environmental program. Seven and a half months later, I was a qualified teacher and, after a summer in the Greek islands, I embarked on what I hoped would be a satisfying and rewarding career.

In becoming a schoolteacher I pass on much of what I learned then, to my students now. They find it hard to believe that I was afraid of my own shadow as a teen, because I exude confidence now.

True art must be an extension of the artist's experience

The philosophy behind each part of this book is a result of my own personal experience. I came to the conclusions based on real moments in my life and the following pages are anecdotal "expressions of my personal experience".

Racism

It should come as no surprise to you that racism saddens me deeply. It makes no sense to me that one individual can pre-judge another on the basis of skin colour or any other physical attribute. I was fortunate as a youngster that even though I was the only visible minority for miles around, I did not experience overt racism until my sixteenth birthday. I remember the experience clearly because it was the evening of my first rock concert. My best friend Damian and I had the worst possible seats for the Van Halen concert at Maple Leaf Gardens, but were ecstatic about the event. We took the subway from suburbia to the concrete jungle of Toronto. The band did not disappoint us and Damian and I were thrilled about our first concert experience. On the voyage home we eagerly discussed the stories we would tell our friends in the morning. Our journey, however, was interrupted on the subway platform when out of nowhere a man and his female companion began yelling at me, "Hey you f*****g packi go home!" My first reaction was to be confused because I thought to myself, " I am going home." But I quickly realized that this individual was going out of his way to humiliate me because of my skin colour. My buddy Damian, a fly-weight boxer, offered a violent solution to the verbal attack, but I quickly ushered him on to our bus to avoid further embarrassment. Damian and I rode silently home the rest of the way. It was an eye-opening experience for both of us. We had been friends for over 12 years and the experience had left us speechless. He was angry and I was hurt. Part of me wished I had let Damian beat the guy to a pulp, but the rest of me knew that that would have solved nothing. I refused to ride the subway ever again. To this day, I cannot understand why someone would expend energy to make another individual feel degraded.

Role Models and Heroes

I have had many role models and heroes in my life but two of them, Dr. David Suzuki and Dr. Jane Goodall, both stand out for a host of reasons.

As a child I was an armchair natural biologist long before I had ever heard of the phrase. I watched every episode of *Mutual of Omaha's Wild Kingdom* and *National Geographic Explorer* with a religious zeal. I vividly remember seeing the geographic coverage of Jane Goodall, then in her early twenties, and her work on the chimpanzees of Gombe. Aside from being beautiful, she had a spiritual aura about her. She believed in her research, in the discoveries she was making and in the dire need for preservation of these magnificent creatures and their habitat. I followed her career and her studies spanning four generations of chimpanzees through the pages of National Geographic and the odd TV documentaries on her field studies. In university I acquired a minor in Social Anthropology and my thesis focused on her research on Pan Troglodytes (chimpanzees).

In 1997, I got to hear Goodall lecture and to this day she is a constant inspiration. After all she has encountered in her lifetime, including the devastation of the African rainforests, the systematic extermination of chimpanzees because of A.I.D.S. research and the consumption of the great apes as bush-meat, she remains optimistic that humans will rectify their behaviour and redeem themselves in the end. When apathy and negative environmental statistics overwhelm me, I think of her words and my motivation is renewed.

Although I have never personally met Dr. David Suzuki, I have considered him my intellectual and sometimes spiritual "guru". His body of written work and television series *The Nature of Things*, have enlightened me and other fellow Canadians on the state of the environment. The award winning documentary series has examined the role of big corporations, government, and modern scientific advancements, in regards to environmental issues. He has always been humble, yet strong in his convictions, and although I perceive him to be highly intelligent, he speaks passionately and simply in a manner that individuals are instantly endeared to him. Like Dr. Goodall, he too, has witnessed the unimaginable destruction of the environment as well as the extreme exploitation of animal species. Yet he also remains hopeful that the intrinsic goodness of humanity will cut through the greed and the planet will be restored to some of its original greatness for future generations to enjoy.

Happiness

In 1997, I had the opportunity to travel to the Island of Bali in the Indonesian Archipelago. After scuba diving around most of the island I ended up on a tiny satellite island called Gilli Meno, which was only about ten square miles in size and had a population of about 1,000 people. There were no hotels, but tiny private huts could be rented close to the beach and were owned and operated by the local families. It was idyllic. Much of my three day stay there was spent lying on the beach and swimming in the surf. Late one afternoon on what was to be my final day I observed a well-fed European boy, about 7 years old, playing on the beach near his parents. He had been completely outfitted with everything a child could desire for a day at the beach: snorkel, mask, fins, pail, shovel and numerous animal-shaped flotation devices. But he was visibly unhappy. He whined and complained and cried for what seemed to be an eternity. His parents acquiesced him with food, more toys and even more food, but to no avail. He seemed determined to be miserable.

At the peak of his disdain a school bell rang in the distance and about three minutes later four local children came squealing down the beach in their school uniform and ran into a ramshackled hut which I had earlier thought to be an outhouse. As it turned out, it was their home and thirtly seconds later they came peeling out of their house stark naked and ran straight into the water, laughing and shrieking with delight. One of the children, a boy of about five, ran behind the shack and reappeared with a piece of garbage. It was something made out of styrofoam and looked like it had once been used as packaging for a beer keg, but it floated and provided hours of pleasure for this exquisite group of children. They splashed and frolicked and made up numerous games using this piece of garbage. Most of the games focused on someone remaining afloat on this make-shift "yacht", while the others tried to capsize him/her. All the while the unhappy European child looked on, but I could see that he was contemplating something. After watching the children for about half an hour, he finally stripped off all of his clothing, discarded his expensive playthings and joined the happy chorus. The Indonesian children accepted him into the group without a second thought and the youngsters played on euphorically until sunset and supper put a halt to their activities. The styrofoam "garbage" boat was carefully stored behind the hut and the children parted ways.

The moral of this story is obvious and I often think of those children who found happiness in the interaction of their siblings, needing nothing but a floating piece of junk to keep them happy (unfortunately I learned three years later that a Japanese Consortium purchased the island and removed all of the islanders in order to turn this "real-estate" into an exclusive golf course for private members. I was deeply saddened and can only hope that the beautiful people who once inhabited this paradise are happy wherever they have been forcibly re-located.)

I, like most Westerners, spent most of my life believing that an abundance of possessions would make me happy, and to that end I worked hard and purchased diligently. I bought Gucci watches, Hilfiger outfits, seven guitars and much more. But the euphoria I experienced at the moment of purchase soon dissipated and I was left feeling empty and confused. I worked more and bought more until my wife at the time and myself had to buy a bigger house to store all of our material items. But the happiness never arrived and finally I began to resent all the "stuff". I felt crowded and disoriented. When my marriage ended, my possessions were divided in half. It was only when I sold or gave away another half of my half that the claustrophobia I was feeling began to subside. I realized that even though I had stripped away most of my material self, I was still the same complete person and I began to feel content.

Touching Wildlife Stories

I have always been truly captivated by animals. When I was five years old I saw a documentary on the plight of Canadian polar bears. Even at that young age I felt sick at the thought that these beautiful creatures, which once lorded over the Arctic regions, were being wiped out for their pelts and by habitat destruction. So I fashioned a make shift donation box with "Save the Polar Bear" emblazoned on the front, and I stood in the foyer of our local Roman Catholic Church after Sunday mass. But the 35 cents I raised was disheartening, and my dad later forbid the activity, for although my efforts impressed him, he explained that there were far more poor people around the world who needed money because they were starving and the polar bears would be looked after by God. I obeyed him, but resented the restriction, because I believed at this young age that humans were the direct cause of the polar bears' situation and as Christ said, "There will always be poor." In any case, I knew then that I had to figure out a way to make my life meaningful in some manner that involved the preservation of animal species.

Many of the greatest moments in my life have involved a wild animal species. Nothing can beat the euphoria of traveling for days, waiting endless hours and then finally witnessing one of God's creatures in its natural environment.

Everybody loves dolphins. They have been ambassadors for not only the ocean's species, but have demonstrated a level of intelligence that elevated the respect that humans have for the animal kingdom. Unfortunately, as humans have often done, the dolphin's ability to learn was exploited in order to entertain us. I detested dolphin shows even as a child, but seeing them up close created a desire to witness them in the natural world and I pursued that goal for over a decade. I obtained my scuba-diving certificate in my early twenties and traveled the Caribbean extensively, diving and searching for dolphins, but they eluded me every time.

It became a running joke between myself and the dolphin world, as I would often arrive on an island, be told that there had been dolphin sightings as recently as the day before and I would end up not seeing a single creature. In 1997, however, on that same trip to Bali, I learned that a large school of dolphins came into a bay on a regular basis to feed off the north side of the island. So I quickly made my way north to the town of Lovina where this blessed event was supposed to occur and I wasn't disappointed. I paid ten dollars to an old fisherman named Wayan, squeezed into his tiny motorized canoe called a "long tail" and headed out into the bay at five o'clock in the morning. The problem was that there were about one hundred other tourists, like myself, who had come to see the same event. When the dolphin pod was sighted about an hour later it was a chaotic sight. Groups of boats would converge on the pod as soon as the playful creatures surfaced and would follow them until they dove down underwater. It was ridiculous. I knew that eco-tourism was becoming popular, but this was insane. I feared that this influx of dolphin enthusiasts would interfere with the animal's feeding patterns. But after much conversation with the locals, I soon learned that as long as the sardines came into the bay, the dolphins would follow. Being chased by the boats just added to the thrill of the hunt and created a dimension of fun for the creatures. But the story does not end here.

Two years later I found myself in Bali again. The reefs around the island were worth visiting a second time and I gravitated toward Lovina and the dolphins once again. I was curious to see whether the tourist traffic was indeed having an impact on the creatures' visitation patterns. The old man Wayan was not around, so I commissioned a different boatman and sure enough at six a.m. sharp, the pod, now larger than two years before, returned to feed and frolic. What interested me even more though was that the number of boats had not increased, and I realized that the Balinese locals had reached a kind of equilibrium between the flotilla of tourists and the dolphin pod. That evening I bumped into Wayan who surprisingly recognized me. He inquired as to whether he could take me out to see the dolphins, but I explained that I had already been out once and he seemed heart- broken. He then tried to convince me that a trip out into the ocean to fish for tuna would be a great experience. I had no real interest in such an excursion but I gave him ten dollars and said that I would meet him in the morning if I happened to be awake. I had no intention of going but I knew that he had too much integrity to take the money even though he was extremely poor.

As fate would have it, when five o'clock the next morning rolled around, I was wide awake staring at the ceiling. So I grabbed my wet suit and scuba mask as I always do when I go out on the ocean, headed down to the beach and jumped in the boat to go fishing with Wayan. It was dark. The ocean was calm and as the long tail sped out toward the horizon, the shoreline quickly disappeared. About an hour into the journey I inquired about our destination, but since Wayan spoke little English, he just nodded, smiled and pointed into oblivion. So I settled back in anticipation of a long ride and watched the sun come up.

About 20 minutes later, out of nowhere, five dolphin pods, with about one hundred members each, surfaced around the boat, frolicking and feasting on sardines. I quickly donned my wetsuit and jumped in. But the creatures seemed wary and maintained a constant distance of about 30 metres from me. I began to think that they were afraid of the boat so I instructed Wayan to take off for about an hour to leave me to swim by myself. He reluctantly departed, shaking his head disapprovingly.

My hunch was right. As soon as the boat was out of sight the dolphins sent four "scouts" to investigate my presence. They swam directly beneath me, soon realized I was harmless and instantly the pods resumed their normal activity as if I wasn't there. It was breathtaking. I swam with these wild and magnificent creatures for over forty-five minutes. There were times when the cacophony of clicks and whistles was so loud that I had to pull my head out of the water. My dream to swim with dolphins, in a natural setting, had finally been realized.

"When the stars threw down their spears
And water'd heaven with their tears,
Did he smile his work to see?
Did he who made the lamb make thee?"
WILLIAM BLAKE

My next animal anecdote takes place underwater, a domain that was virtually free from human explorers until Jacques Cousteau invented the self contained underwater breathing apparatus. Scuba-diving is my favourite past-time. The feeling of weightlessness and the sensory deprivation of sound and smell has always led me to believe that it is the closest thing to space travel that I'll ever experience. Like most outdoor activities, conducted properly, scuba-diving is an ideal form of eco-tourism. Travelers can only trespass for as long they have oxygen and leave only bubbles behind; of course this is only true if divers solicit dive operations that use permanent moorings, maintain neutral buoyancy to avoid bumping into the fragile coral systems, refrain from touching the fragile reef, and spear-fishing.

The underwater world is magnificent. The colours are exhilarating and the creatures indescribable. I have swum with sea turtles (my all time favourite member of God's creations), been surrounded by over a thousand barracuda and been bitten by a triggerfish, but shark encounters are always life-defining moments. Once, on a dive in Cuba, I stuck my head into a cave sixty feet under the ocean and saw a huge shark's tail in the darkness. I could not resist the urge to touch this beautiful creature and since I knew that the dangerous end of the shark was deep inside the cave, I gently stroked the sleeping beast. It felt like silk, made out of sandpaper. I thought to myself, that only God could take the softest and coarsest of materials and mesh them together to form perfection. While I was marveling at this, the creature woke up, quickly turned around and sped by me through the entrance to the cave. What I first envisioned to be a 6-foot creature, based on the tail-size, actually turned out to be a pregnant 12-foot nurse shark. She stealthily cruised around me while I hyperventilated into my regulator, but she showed no real signs of aggression. Satisfied that I posed no threat to her, she retreated back into her hiding spot and as I looked into her eyes, I could imagine her thinking, "silly human, go back to the surface where you belong." And so I did ... as I was not willing to argue with a shark that was twice my size. I learned a few weeks later that a 14-year-old boy had been drowned by a nurse shark who had clamped onto his body with a vice-like grip so strong, that in order to remove the creature from the body, the spinal cord of the shark had to be severed. Since then I have adopted the environmentally friendly policy of "Look, but don't touch."

"I want to hold your hand ..."

LENNON AND MCCARTNEY

We are often inundated with negative accounts about the state of the world, but the next story, like the previous one, demonstrates the beauty of God's creations and the success that humans can achieve when they work together to protect them. In the late 1990's I once again found myself in South East Asia, this time trekking through India and on through Thailand. I learned early on when traveling that the best information about a destination comes from somebody who has recently traversed there. So I networked as much as possible and made many new friends while exchanging stories.

Late one night while I was talking to a group of university students from Britain, a young couple from Australia pulled up a few chairs and began telling this fantastic tale of how they had seen orangutans in a jungle region on the island of Sumatra. They spoke of a successful program where young orangutans were being rehabilitated and reintroduced back into their natural environment.

Even though I had only ten days left before I had to return home, I knew that I had to go and see this magical place for myself. So I siphoned all the information I could from them and armed only with a map drawn on a paper napkin and a rough idea that the journey would take approximately three days, I began a trek to a tiny village called Bohorok on the northern tip of Sumatra. Five days later, after a sixteen hour minivan ride through Penang, Malaysia, a twelve hour ferry ride to the western most province of Indonesia and a twelve hour nail-biting taxi ride in the dead of night, I arrived at what appeared to be a four-unit trailer park decorated with Christmas lights in the middle of a tropical jungle. The gracious owners of the "hotel" assured me that we were indeed amongst the orang-utans. I awoke early the next morning, had a quick breakfast and geared up for the trek into the jungle, (quickly pausing to remove a large, hairy spider, the size of a compact disc, from my shorts). After what seemed an eternity, through air thick with humidity, we arrived at a tiny base camp where Indonesian volunteers explained the process of orangutan conservation and rehabilitation. Station One was a quarantine where baby orangutans, newly snatched from captivity, were quarantined and nursed back to health. They were often malnourished, permanently scarred from beatings by their human owners or even maimed from the shackles of captivity. 30% died within the first month. Those who survived underwent an intensive, but loving training session during which they were taught the fundamentals of orangutan life. After about two years and many guided forages into the jungle, candidates were then released at Station Two, about four miles from base camp. The goal at this stage was for the orangutans to exist as self-sufficiently as possible. But twice daily, fortified milk and bananas were brought to a platform by a volunteer to monitor and ensure proper health. It was during these feedings that a limited number of outsiders were permitted to witness this extraordinary conservation/restoration effort.

I told the head researcher about my minor in Anthropology and studies in Primatology and was graciously given a behind-the-scenes tour of the program. After that, I began the arduous one-hour journey to the platform at Station 2, when it happened. While I was focusing most of my energies fighting the urge to pass out in the heat and maintain a sure foot on the slippery trail, I felt a soft and gentle hand clasp mine. I looked down, and to my disbelief a six-year-old male orangutan had reached out to say hello and subsequently steal the water bottle out of my back pocket. My guide explained that he had been released almost two years ago and must have mistaken me for an Indonesian volunteer because of my similar colouring. Whatever the reason, it was by far one of the most memorable moments of my lifetime. When we finally reached the feeding station, I was treated to the sight of five reintegrated orangutans, including a captive-born mother who had been reintroduced into the wild and her newborn baby. It was exhilarating. For me, Bohorok and its orangutan conservation program represents the greatness we can achieve when they strive to repair the damage of our explosive and exploitative domination of the earth.

Conclusion

So what's the point? Well, I want my children's grandchildren, and generations beyond them to be able to see orangutans, dolphins, sharks and every other member of the earth's menagerie in the beauty of their natural habitat too. I hope that they write a book about their adventures traveling around the world, diving on coral reefs and trekking through lush healthy rain-forests. And I believe that this can come true if the philosophy you have just read about is embraced by millions of people worldwide.

Unfortunately, we live in a world where the majority of people just don't care. In some nations, they dine on shark-fin soup, made out of the fins of sharks, which are hacked off the bodies of these beautiful creatures. The bodies are then dumped overboard, and the sharks, still alive, die slowly at the bottom of the ocean (I'm willing to bet that the person eating this ridiculously priced soup couldn't tell the difference between the real thing and a broth made out of the leather from the bottom of my shoe). In our backyard in Canada, old growth forests are being chopped down at an alarming rate to satiate the needs of the lumber and paper industries.

Now I am not egotistical enough to claim that Empowerists are going to save the earth. But I think that if enough people really subscribe to the basic philosophy of this book, and if they in turn convince the mega-corporations that their methods of money making need to be drastically altered, a balance can be reached and maintained between humans and Mother Earth.

I'd like to close with a true story that I viewed on the television during the writing of this book. It chronicled the life of an African-American homeless man who decided to turn his life around at a fairly ripe old age. He stopped panhandling one day and began collecting recyclable containers, such as aluminum cans and plastic bottles. He would drop these off at recycling depots for 10 cents apiece, and use the money to eke out a meagre living. One day he recruited another local homeless person, and offered him five cents for every can he would collect for him. This "business" expanded, and now ten years later, he employs over 40 people at any given time who collect thousands of containers every night from the streets and waste receptacles of New York city. He earns over 100,000 U.S. dollars a year from the materials that people carelessly throw away and then donates most of his income to homeless shelters in the area. He is still homeless himself, but by choice. Every moment of his life he is empowering himself, the disenfranchised people around him and Mother Earth beneath him.

EPILOGUE

About a month before this book was sent to press I got the opportunity to travel to Baja California in Mexico. The goal was to scuba dive in the Sea of Cortez which is known world-wide for whale-sharks, manta rays, hammerhead sharks and sea-lions. On my second day of diving I was lucky enough to swim with a fifteen foot manta ray for 20 minutes. She was beautiful. She liked the bubbles that were expelled from my scuba regulator and she passed numerous times through them. Two weeks into the trip I also got the chance to swim with dolphins again as well as a large group of pilot whales. A large male pilot whale swam under me three or four times to investigate my presence and appeared to want to play. Unfortunately, I was snorkeling at the time and did not have the means to accept his offer (not to mention that I was very intimidated by his size). After speaking to many of the divemasters in the area it became very clear that the populations of these whales were increasing due to the world-wide ban on whaling. This is concrete proof that humankind can indeed have a huge positive impact on the natural world if there are concerted efforts. But there is dark side to this story too. None of the dive operations were seeing hammerhead sharks, even though this was the peak breeding season in the Sea of Cortez. The local divemasters theorized that "finning" for the Japanese shark-fin soup industry was slowly wiping out this species. I was told that eight years ago as many as four hundred sharks would school in the area but numbers have steadily declined and only thirty were seen last year. I was told of other horrific stories of manta rays being captured too, and the tip of their wings being cut off to pass as shark fins. The point is obvious. The state of the environment is directly linked to humankind's desire to protect or destroy our world. **Do you want to be part of the problem or part of the solution?**

PART III

The Power of T.E.N.

THE EMPOWERISTS' NETWORK

The Empowerists' Network

"We need to recruit a contingency of people who will strive to not only live their lives with a minimal impact on the environment but who will work to undo the damage that others have incurred on Mother Earth."

CHRISTOPHER MARK D'SOUZA,
Founder of the Empowerists' Network

It is my dream that Empowerism will expand into a grass roots movement. Once a person has adopted its philosophy and incorporated many of its ideals into their lifestyle then networking with other Empowerists is an obvious and logical progression. "What we've got right now is a corporate culture that places on the highest pedestal the mercantile standard by which everything is judged. If you can't turn everything into money, which makes the rich richer and the corporations' cash registers ring, then it's not adequately valued", says consumer advocate Ralph Nader.

Nader's solution is simply to create a civic culture instead, one that is a sensitive membrane for a whole range of values other than just mercantile ones, the personal average income and corporate profits. Nader lists such values as health, safety, the impact on posterity, the preservation of other living things and developing a qualitative measurement of our quality of life (Gordon). When two empowered individuals work together their positive productive output does not simply double. Because they are empowered, their potential is infinite. A network of Empowerists, who communicate regularly, set environmental goals and then meet to execute their ideas would be ideal.

T.E.N. : The Empowerists' Network – A network will be set up on the Internet by which Empowerists can log on at www.empowerism.net and access information about the group's activities. The network itself will be comprised of groups of community chapters who meet regularly, plan and carry out activities that empower themselves and the environment. Successful endeavors and the methods that made them possible should be recorded and logged on the website so that others can access the data and reconstruct the activity in their local area. The Empowerists' Network subscribes to the philosophy of most environmentalists that Earth Day events should occur on a regular basis and not just once a year.

Events should include:

1. Environmental restoration/clean up of local parks, streets, rivers, creeks, forests, wetlands etc.
2. Lobbying local governments about policy to improve environmental conditions.
3. Monitoring local companies and industries in regards to their environmental practices.

BIBLIOGRAPHY

Gordon, Anita. Suzuki, David. *It's a matter of Survival.* Toronto: Stoddart Publishing Co. Limited, 1990.

Lanza, Robert. *One World: The Health and Survival of the Human Species in the 21st Century.* New Mexico: Health Press, 1996.

Rolston, Holmes. *Philosophy Gone Wild: Environmental Ethics.* New York: Prometheus Books, 1989.

Southwick, Charles H. *Global Ecology In Human Perspective.* New York: Oxford University Press, Inc.,1996.

Suzuki, David. Dressel, Holly. *From Naked Ape to Superspecies.* Toronto: Stoddart Publishing Co. Limited, 1999.

Please feel free to contact me with any
questions, comments or suggestions
regarding the book or
The Empowerists' Network at

chrismarkdsouza@hotmail.com